Why the Coyote Yelps: Fifth Grade Pourquoi Tales

Mrs. Heavin's Class

2017

Saskatoon Public School Division
ISBN-13: 978-0968471067
ISBN-10: 0968471064

Images from depositphotos.com

Meet Our Authors

Ar Macin Nagra Malik

Jennifer Ly

Livy Arndd

Peyton

Emily

Logan

Beck

Caden Kucher

Jeny

ABBas-ali

Ruoyi

Usayd Ali

Addan

Tavin Lorenz

Madison Hong

Ava Reber Hi

Alexandra Zhu

Nini Li

Josh Purdie

Katie Prosky

Hailey Jue

Aidric

Rubic

Osher

Stromberg

Foreword

By Jennifer Berthelot & Amy Heavin

This collaborative book is a culminating project for a grade 5 traditional literature unit of study. Students and teachers worked together to learn about the characteristics of traditional literature. The students were assigned a Pourquoi tale writing assignment where they were to demonstrate their understanding of various elements of writing and traditional literature.

"Pourquoi tales - or "why" tales, in an English translation of the French word – answer a question or explain how animals, plants, or humans were created and why they have certain characteristics."
- Dr. Donna Norton, *Through the Eyes of a Child: An Introduction to Children's Literature*

During the first writing lesson, we discussed the fear each child felt about being judged for their work. We chatted about growth and fixed mindsets and worked with the kids to help them understand that they were all writers with a story in them that was worthy of sharing. We helped them understand that their writing was not expected to be perfect in draft form and that it was all about getting their ideas down and refining them as they moved through the process. Following a lesson modeling the first stages of the writing process, students worked on their Pourquoi tales to explain why something had come to be. Teachers gave students a choice to work together or alone on their stories and all students selected their topics.

Once the students had completed their rough drafts, both teachers spent time conferencing with students working through their stories to ensure they had successfully communicated their ideas using strong organizational structure. Students were encouraged to find their unique voices, experiment with word choice, smooth out their fluency, work on editing their work and preparing it for the collaborative book.

Students learned how to access the thesaurus on the word processor to help them select more interesting words to place within their work. When conferencing, teachers helped students work on clarifying their ideas with elaboration strategies. To improve fluency students were encouraged to play with word choice, patterns, transitions and the structure of their sentences. Students were invited to take ownership of their writing by fully embracing the use of their personal voices. Finally, spell check and Grammarly were used to help edit the work. (**This book has not been professionally edited**.) Students read their final submissions and had to sign off on their work, understanding that the final draft was their responsibility.

For our students who were working through EAL programs, we worked with them to create a short tale in English and then consulted with our EAL teacher, caretaker, fellow students, and Google translate to present their stories in their first language as well. **Please forgive us if there are errors but we felt strongly that these students have a chance to contribute successfully in both languages**. The Arabic translator was not working properly so this student neatly wrote the translation and prepared it for scanning. The Chinese translations also required additional work as these are not precise tools.

Our cover was designed using a paid image from depositphotos.com and canva.com. Students were presented with three cover design options, and they voted on the winning design. The interior design was formatted in Microsoft Word and illustrations by the students were integrated into the design and then exported to PDF. All of the files were combined into our final book project. Once the book files had been loaded into the dashboard of our publishing account, the kids watched as we flipped through the virtual version of the book identifying what we had left to do or correct. After making the required changes, we ordered a proof copy of the physical book to approve and then placed our book order from Amazon for our book launch celebration.

We hope you enjoy these stories with your children and continue to nourish their desire to write and communicate with the written word.

Acknowledgements

We would like to extend our gratitude to Mr. Kent Ritchie and Mr. Salha Wahba and Nini Li for helping us read over the text in other languages. Also, thanks goes to Veronica Baker and Kevin Epp who worked quickly to ensure we could proceed with this project and complete it in a timely manner.

Dedication

This book is dedicated to kids around the world. You are all writers and you have important stories to share with the world! Find your voice and write!

Table of Contents

Why the Coyote Yelps

By Mrs. Heavin's Grade 5 Class

The following story is the Pourquoi tale that we created together as we modelled the early stages of the writing process with the students.

In a land far away, where the towering, emerald green pine trees reached for the clouds, there lived a coyote named Chris. Chris spent his days chasing squirrels and remaining elusive as coyotes always do.

Chris would stroll quietly through the forest. He could hear the sounds of all the other wildlife in the woods. Birds would sing. Squirrels would chatter and bark. Even the smaller animals like snakes made their own sounds. Chris longed to find his own voice, but every time he opened his mouth nothing came out.

Chris was so quiet that sometimes he would accidently sneak up on other animals who were bigger than him. He would startle them, and because they were afraid, they would attack. Startling the other animals didn't help him make friends either.

Chris had no other coyote buddies and he had no way of finding them because had no voice, no way to ask the other animals if they had seen other coyotes, and no way to communicate with his kind even if he could find them. Chris spent his evenings looking up at the moon in the sky, wondering if it was lonely too.

He yearned to find his true love, but he had no way to beckon his mate. He had almost gotten used to the idea of being alone. He was also hungry, and he could never find any good food to eat. Chris was kind of lazy too, and he would spend time under the trees dreaming about ways he could trick his prey to come to him.

Over time, Chris became increasingly more miserable because he couldn't connect with any other animals, so he decided to ask the moon for help. He had overheard two bears talking one day about the magical powers of the moon.

One night, when the moon was shining brightly across the tree tops, Chris decided to signal the moon for help. He threw his head up high, started prancing around on his feet, and clawing at trees. The moon did nothing. Chris continued. Still, the moon remained still and quiet. Chris was desperate to be noticed. He continued his antics for hours.

Suddenly, in anger, the moon rotated quickly and flung a few solid moon rocks at Chris to make him stop!

The moon rocks hit Chris brutally in the neck and face. Surprisingly, Chris began to yelp and howl at the moon because he was in great pain.

His yelps and howls attracted all of the other lone coyotes in the area. The coyotes gathered to see what the commotion was all about. Instead, they found themselves looking at one of their own kind in distress. The lone coyotes ran to help Chris. Instead, they found themselves pelted by moon rocks too. The forest was now filled with the sounds of coyotes yelping and howling at the moon, pleading for it to stop throwing rocks at them.

The dawn of the new day begins to push the angry moon out of the sky. And as the day begins the coyotes celebrate their new friendships and voices. And from this day forward, all coyotes yelp, howl and travel in packs.

Why the Tiger Has Stripes

By Aidric Rubic

Long ago in an Asian grassland lived a tiger named Stripes. Stripes lived with his mother. He was made fun of by the other tigers that roamed the area. They would laugh at him because his name was Stripes, but he didn't have any stripes. He was also smaller than the other tigers, which made him a target. He had no friends and no siblings to play with so he was isolated and miserable.

One day when he was being bullied, he ran away because he felt like he didn't matter. He wandered over the tall hills through the rainforest and into the forbidden swamp. He was lost, scared and alone. All he wanted was his mother. As he wandered, he heard voices coming from above him. He followed the voices which lead him to an opening in a swampy area. He looked up through the opening into the sky where the voices were coming from and realized that the voices were coming from the Sky Gods. He began to cry.

The Sky Gods stopped talking because they heard Stripes crying on the earth below them. The Sky Gods took mercy on Stripes and asked how they could help him.

Stripes explained his situation. He told the Sky Gods that he wanted to find his way home and he wanted things to change, so he didn't get picked on anymore.

The Sky Gods gathered to hold a Miracle Meeting. They called upon Stripes to share their decision. They told him they would do three things to assist him. First, they would help him to find his way home. They would draw a map of the land on his fur so he would never lose his way again. Secondly, they would make him big and strong so that he wouldn't get picked on. He would never feel like he had to leave his home again. Finally, the map they would draw on his fur would make him unique and special. All the other tigers would want to be just like him. And so Stripes' transformation into a "real tiger" began.

The Gods draw the map on his fur using sacred swamp mud and explain how to get home safely. They also make him powerful and strong. Stripes catches his reflection in a nearby lake and is excited because he looks so beautiful and sturdy. He also realizes that his name now matches his appearance.

When Stripes returns to his home, the other tigers gather around him jealous of his unique look. Within days, all the tigers have followed Stripes' fashion trend and painted one another with distinctive stripes. Each tiger's stripes are unique like human fingerprints. This is why the tiger has his beautiful stripes to this very day.

Why the Zebra Has Stripes

By Abbas Ali

In a savanna far away there was a herd of horses that worked very hard for a Chief. These horses had never been wild and were raised as part of the Chief's herd. One day when they were hauling water and plowing fields, they saw wild horses running in the fields off in the distance.

As the working horses looked on, they were overwhelmed with a sense of sadness. They longed to be free. They watched as the free range horses thundered through water and stretched their legs. Their manes waved in the wind.

The working horses wanted to join the free range horses, but they knew the chief wouldn't let them go. They didn't like how the Chief was treating them. The working horses thought that perhaps they could sneak out and join the free range horses in the evenings and return before the Chief even knew they were missing.

When it was dark, the work horses snuck out of their paddock. However, they didn't make it far because they got caught by the Royal Guards. These Royal Guards told the Chief what happened. The Chief was furious, and for punishment, he assigned them extra work. The work horses were miserable.

One day when they were working in the fields, they saw the Great Goddess of the Hunt. The Great Goddess asked them why they were feeling so unhappy. The work horses explained their situation to the Goddess and told her they longed to be free.

The Great Goddess said that she would help them escape. But first, she needed them to steal some of the Chief's paint. With a new sense of hope, the horses brought her the paint. The Great Goddess used the paint to camouflage the work horses with black stripes, so they were unrecognizable to the Chief.

Next, the Goddess helped the disguised horse sneak past the Royal Guards. Once they were free, they thundered through the water and played all day in the open fields. Their manes waved in the wind. It was quite the sight.

To complete their escape, they change their name to Zebras. They stay together in a strong and protective herd, and they live happily ever after right under the nose of the mean Chief.

And this is why the Zebra has its beautiful stripes.

Why the Panda Has Black Eyes

By Jerry Cui

Once there was a fat panda who was always bullied at school because he looked like a penguin and a zebra. He would get in fights with other kids because they made fun of him, and one day he ended up with two black eyes!

However, when he had these black eyes, everyone was scared of him because he looked tough and mean. He liked it because everyone left him alone.

Panda decided he would keep the black eyes so he would not be bullied anymore. He tried a few things and decided that he would put marker on his face to make his eyes stay black.

Before long, the marker would no longer wash off and Panda kept his black eyes forever. This is why the panda has black eyes! But I think that the panda's black eyes are cute.

从前有一个肥胖的熊猫，因为看起来像一只企鹅和斑马，所以他总是在学校被人欺负。有一天熊猫打架得到了两只黑眼睛!

然而，他有这些黑眼睛，每个人都害怕他，因为他看起来很凶猛。

他很高兴，因为每个人都会躲着他。

熊猫决定他会保持黑眼睛，那样他就不会被欺负了。他尝试了几件事情，决定把彩笔涂在脸上，使他的眼睛保持黑色。

不久之后，标记就洗不掉了，熊猫永远保持黑眼睛。这就是熊猫黑眼睛的来历! 但我认为熊猫的黑眼睛很可爱。

Why the Snowy Owl Has Big Eyes

By: Alexandra Zhu and Madison Hong

Long, long ago there was an owl named Snowfall, but her family called her Snowy. She was as white as snow and silent as a mouse, but she had trouble seeing. Beautiful as she was, her eyes were extremely tiny. She lived in an old, renovated polar bears den. Her home was deep in the snow on the cold tundra.

Every day she wished she had bigger eyes because she had trouble seeing. Snowy was often bullied by the other animals because of her small eyes. She also could not see her prey on the land from the dizzying heights at which she flew. She would utter low, raspy hoots in despair, repeatedly, wishing for things to be different. She did her best to hunt small mammals such as rabbits, rodent, and other birds despite her poor eyesight.

Snowy also had to be wary of foxes, jaegers, dogs, wolves and large birds because she was their prey. However, she did have one special friend Whisper the wolf. Snowfall and Whisper often traveled the woods together warning one another of possible danger. Whisper was very aware that Snowy struggled with her eye sight and wanted to help Snowy see better.

Luckily for Snowy, Whisper had once saved a magical fairy from being attacked by her wolf pack.   This fairy had granted Whisper one magical wish that she had not used yet. Whisper thought long and hard about it and had decided to use the wish to help Snowy see better.

The two of them traveled together to the magical border where the tundra meets the forest. This boarder repelled anyone who tried to cross unless they had permission from a magical creature. Whisper had permission. The two of them crossed the border together and entered the Enchanted Forest.

Whisper took Snowy to look for the fairy ring to have her wish granted at last. They found the fairy ring, stepped inside, and at once, the fairy appeared. "I wish my friend Snowy and her family could hunt in the dark and have amazing eye sight. This would allow them to easily spot their prey from high in the sky," Whisper declared. The fairy happily granted the wish, and the two friends returned to the tundra.

While Snowy sleeps in the day, she dreams about hunting at night. When she awakes, her entire life has changed. She looks at the ice mirror on the wall and sees her enormous new eyes in her reflection.

This is why, from that day forward, all Snowy owls have big, beautiful and powerful eyes.

Why the Timber Wolf Has Sharp Teeth

By Ava Reber

Long ago, there was a gray wolf named Leona. She roamed the Rocky Mountains because solo roaming was one of her biggest hobbies. She loved the sight of all the slowly falling snow on a warm winter day. Leona was one of the little wolves that loved to be on her own. Leona didn't take a fancy to the other gray wolves because she was more timid, and it was for this reason they all teased and shunned her. Even her family shunned her. This made her feel like she didn't belong with the rest of the wolves.

One day as she was out on her daily walk through the mountains, Balto and Gene showed up to tease and claw at her. Dottie, Rylan, and Daniel showed up to protect Leona but the bullies continued and didn't care about being caught or stopped. Dottie, Rylan, and Daniel were the only wolves who didn't shun Leona. Because of their kindness, Leona cared for them a great deal.

The next day, Leona was out for her walk when she was approached by Gene. Today was an important day because the pack's alpha female, Kiki was selecting their alpha male. The alpha male and alpha female would become the leaders of the pack. With an alpha female already in place, today the pack was selecting the alpha male because without one there could be chaos. Balto, Daniel, and Rylan, all being older, were trying out for this essential role, so that left Gene alone to get into trouble. Dottie was ill, so she was home resting.

It was snowing heavily as Leona made her way along a tree line, she was asking herself, "Why would they pick the worst day for Alpha tryouts?"

When Gene showed up along the tree line he was alone. He appeared bothered by something, perhaps his exclusion from the tryouts, and he took his frustration out on Leona.

He began scratching at Leona for no reason in particular. Leona thought to herself about the fact that there would be no one to help her today and she would have to fight to protect herself.

As Gene attacked her, she scratched and clawed, digging through his skin and thrashing through his fur. All of a sudden fueled by fear, she lost control of herself and kept hitting him even though he was begging for her to stop. He was in so much pain that he was yelping. He got up and pushed through the pain, continuing to hack at Leona, giving her scars that would stay throughout her lifetime. They slashed and clawed until they were out of breath, but Leona was out of control realizing that she had so much power.

Leona hit his face, causing him to go blind in the one eye. "That does it," Gene said in a low, scary voice. Leona had never heard this tone before. A cold, sharp shock was sent through her body, as she felt her sins crawling on her back, causing her to go as still as a statue. She was terrified. As Gene slashed at Leona, she backed away, falling down the mountainside. Her mouth was cut, and splinters of the broken trees caused her jaw bone to pierce through her gums. Her bone stabbed through the flesh giving her sharp studs outside of her gums. 42 piercings were replaced with bone. Leona lay unconscious at the bottom of the mountains, and when she woke up she was back in her den surrounded by Dottie, Rylan, and Daniel.

As her mouth healed, the bones remained as teeth, and that is why to this day all wolves have sharp teeth. They allow them to eat prey and defend themselves. As you know, Leona was a nice girl and only stood her ground when she had no other choice. This is the true nature of wolves. They are only fierce if provoked and now they have sharp teeth to defend themselves.

Why the Ladybug Has Dots

By Ruoyi Dan

A long time ago, in the colorful garden there was a bug. The bug believed she was not beautiful. She felt very sad because she really wanted to be a pretty bug. The bug went to find Mrs. Heavin because Mrs. Heavin has magic.

Bug says, "I believe I'm not beautiful. Can you help me?"

"Sure," Mrs. Heavin then sprinkled black magic on the bug's back which created dots on her back.

Next, Mrs. Heavin told the bug she needed a new name to go with her new beauty.

"How about we call you Ladybug?"

The bug agrees and loves her new name.

The ladybug thought she was so beautiful now and she wanted to have black dots forever. From then on, the ladybug always had black dots on her back and she felt very beautiful.

This is why ladybugs have beautifully dotted backs.

很久以前，在五颜六色的花园里有一个昆虫。她感到非常伤心，因为她想成为一个漂亮的昆虫。传说霍文夫人有魔法，所以昆虫历经千辛万苦找到了霍文夫人。 昆虫说："我认为我不漂亮，你可以帮我吗？"

"当然可以，"霍文夫人想了想然后在昆虫背后撒上了黑色的魔法，创造了一些黑色的点在昆虫身上。

然后，霍文夫人告诉她，她需要一个新的名字去符合她新的美丽。

"我们要不叫你七星瓢虫？"七星瓢虫同意并喜欢她的新名字。

七星瓢虫认为她现在很漂亮，她想要永远有黑点。从那时起，七星瓢虫的背部总是有黑点。

这就是为什么七星瓢虫有美丽的点缀。

Why the Pig Has a Curly Tail

By Beck Humber, Peyton, and Armaan Nagra

Long ago in a cornfield far away, there was a pig named Paul. He loved his straight tail, but he felt like he was a little boring looking, so he told his Mom, "I feel too ordinary looking."

She said, "You look exactly like you are supposed to look."

His mom's answer did not leave him satisfied. He kept expressing his feelings about his appearance. Finally, she got fed up and said, "THAT'S ENOUGH Paul, and you look fine! Go outside and find something else to do!"

Paul headed outside and climbed the biggest, tallest tree that he could find. He was way up at the top, way higher than his mom says he should climb. At first, the wind began to whisper and gently moved the tree. Paul began to sway high in the tree tops.

The wind grew stronger. There was a storm approaching from the north. The clouds were shaking and rumbling. The strong wind pushed him off the tree and into the air. As he fell, his tail got caught in the tree branches. Paul kept falling, his tail kept stretching, and as he hit the hard ground, his tail was released and sprung back to his bottom. And just like the ribbon on a Christmas gift, Paul's tail looked like a curly fry.

Paul's tail was beautifully curled, and the other pigs commented that his tail looked amazing. Paul created a stretching machine and began curling all of their tails. He started a piggy fashion trend.

And this is why the pig has a curly tail.

Why the Fox Has a White Tipped Tail

By: Jennifer Ly and Hailey Rye

Long, long ago, in a den far away, there lived a fox named Whisper. He was lucky because he had white paws while other foxes had orange paws. The foxes made fun of Whisper because he was different from everyone else. Winter had come to the area and Whisper was getting colder each day. Whisper knew he had to hunt to survive, but every time he went out to try, he had to run back to his den because it was too cold and he was so scared of the predators.

"I'm hungry. I know I'm a good hunter but I'm only a cub, and I can easily be hunted by the great eagle and ferocious bear. I'm not supposed to be outside but my parents died trying to protect me when I was three."

After trying for days to hunt, a great and powerful God sent a magical mouse to help him.   The mouse skittered into his den saying, "Here are some juicy fruits you may eat, but once you eat, I will guide you to a steaming hot spring that you can bathe in to warm up."

After 15 miles of walking, they finally arrived at the hot spring. Whisper told the mouse, "I'm tired of walking but it's worth it. I haven't bathed since winter came because it's so cold."

Whisper jumped into the hot spring. After a couple of minutes, he began to warm up. His head was still cold, so he dove deeply into the warm water. However, foxes do not like to get their tails wet so while Whisper swam and warmed up, he kept his tail poking out of the hot spring. He swam in the hot spring for so long that his tail was kissed with frost from the steam of the warm water.

When he got out of the hot spring, the magical mouse had disappeared into thin air, and the tip of Whisper's tail was white and sparkly because the frost

had formed thickly on his tail. Once he had warmed up, he went back into his den very satisfied for deep sleep.

When he woke up and came out of his den, all the other foxes surrounded Whisper. Pointing at his frosted tail with their paws, they asked, "Where did you get that?" "That's so cool!"

He curiously looked at his tail wondering what they were talking about. Happily, he remembered where the hot spring was and showed all the other foxes where the hot spring was. Since they were so excited, they all dove in one by one. Of course, since foxes don't like their tails wet everyone dove and swam as the frost formed on their tail tips.

And this is why foxes have white tipped tails.

Why the Dolphin Squeaks

By Katie Prosky and Emily Rueb

A long time ago there was a beautiful young dolphin named Aqua. She was a lovely, joyful, adventurous dolphin who always looked forward to discovering new things. Aqua did not fit in with the other dolphins because she was a little bit different. She didn't like to do what the other dolphins liked to do. Her mother always said that being different meant she was special.

One day she saw a bright white fishing boat in the distance. Curiosity overtook her, and she felt drawn to discover it. She slowly and carefully swam out to the boat. Unfortunately, the people on the boat were illegally fishing in a dolphin zone.

Aqua got caught in the fishing net and could not come up to the surface to breathe. She started to panic, and her throat hit the bottom of the fishing boat. When the fishermen pulled up the net, they saw a young dolphin with an injured throat. The fishermen quickly rushed Aqua to the nearest animal hospital. Even though they were fishing illegally, they cared about the dolphins.

The next morning when Aqua woke up, she was in an aquarium with other dolphins. Her throat was still injured, and her vocal chords were damaged beyond repair. When she swam up to the surface, she saw the deep blue ocean off in the distance and longed for her home. She tried calling out to her parents for help, but all that came out was a loud eerie squeak. This injury would never heal.

Years later, when she was released back into the wild, she had a family and children of her own. All of her family members had also inherited this eerie ability to squeak. This eerie squeak was passed down to all future generations. The dolphin has adapted to use this squeak to communicate with others in their pod.

And that is why the dolphin squeaks to this day.

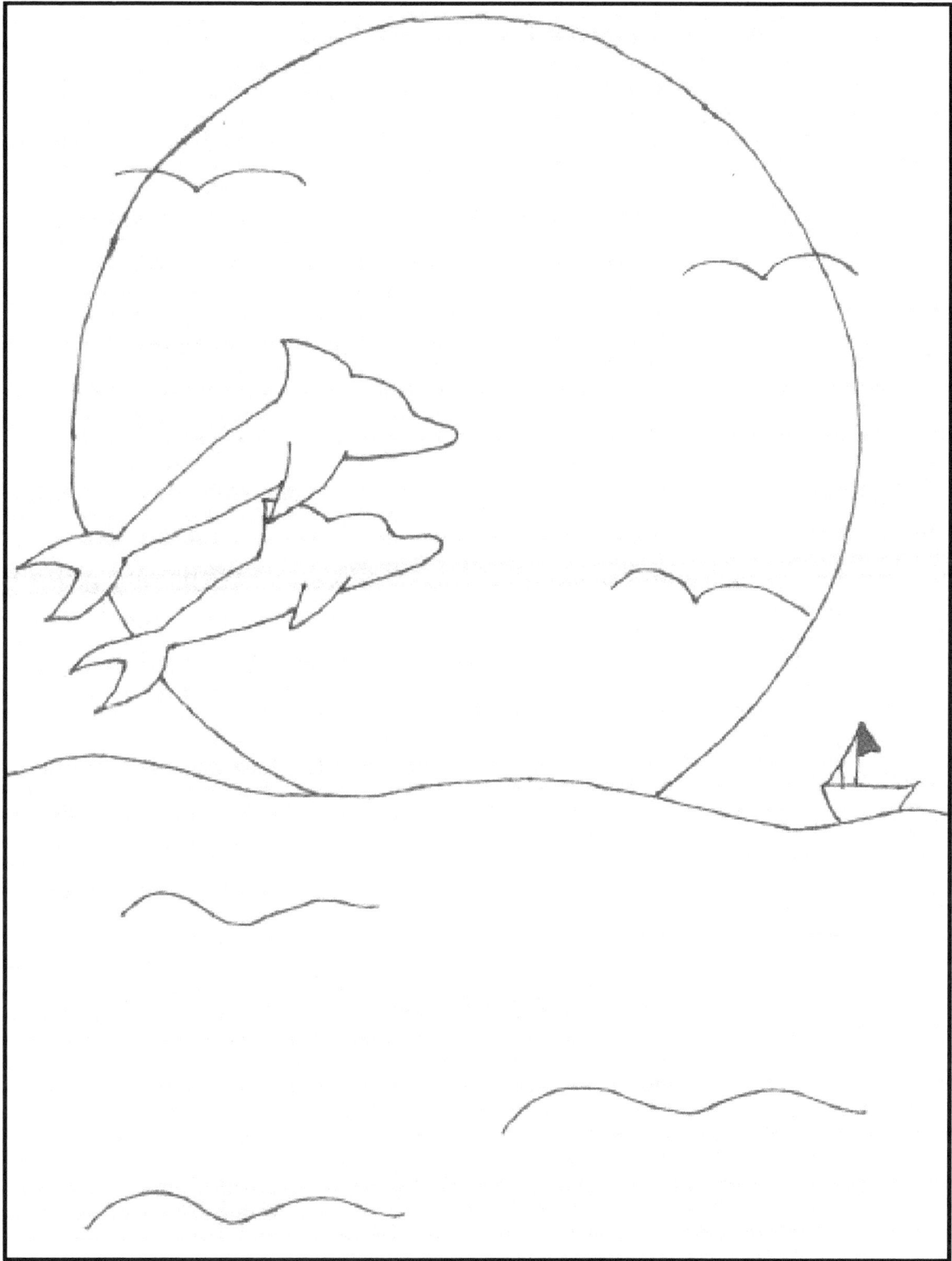

Why the White-Tailed Deer Has Antlers

By Livy Arnold

Long ago, there lived a deer named Bryan. He lived in a hardwood forest with his family where the broadleaf trees grew. He passed his long days by walking in the gorgeous forest. He was always talking to other animals. Sometimes he would play with his sister Leila. Bryan did tricks to make the little ones laugh. One day Bryan got so curious about something that he became distracted and walked somewhere where he shouldn't have gone.

There were large spiders in sticky webs hanging on the trees over the path. On the ground, there were crunchy, dead leaves with acorns on top. He realized that he had stumbled into the forbidden forest where nothing grows. Bryan got spooked and accidentally bumped into a magical tree. The tree was very old; it had nothing on it. The branches were going out in all different directions. The tree was in the center of the forbidden forest.

Bryan backed away very slowly. He looked up at the tree and was stunned to see how scary it was. He stood there in fear staring at the tree. The tree noticed Bryan and got angry at him. He started to wave his branches around trying to scare Bryan into leaving him alone. Bryan screamed so loud in fear that you could hear cries for miles.

This noise made the tree enraged with anger. You see, the tree did not want to be discovered, and Bryan was making a huge scene! The tree started to toss his branches at him. The sticks got stuck by Bryan's ears. In pain, Bryan ran off in the direction he came from to find his buddies.

His friends heard his cries and followed the sounds to find him. They were shocked to see he had sticks coming out from behind his ears.

"What happened?" They asked in surprise.

Instead of explaining, he took his friends to the magical tree to show them. The arrival of more deer did not make the tree happy. He was even more infuriated because Bryan had now shown the tree to more animals, but the tree did not want to be known to the rest of the world. Finally, the tree got so mad he tossed his remaining branches at Bryan and his friends. In terror, they all fled the forest in pain. Each of them now has branches piercing their skulls.

And this is why the white-tailed deer has antlers.

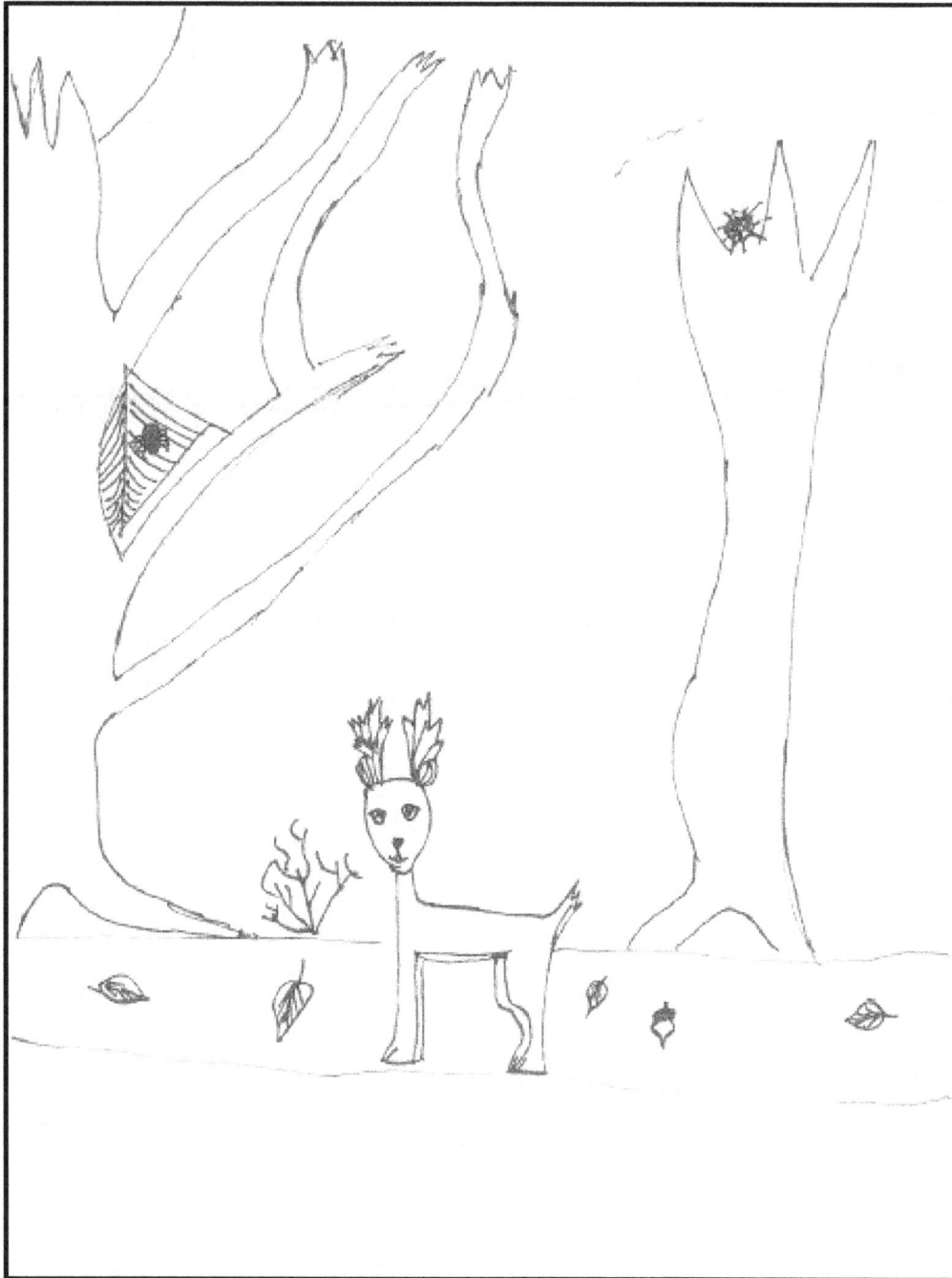

Why the Rhino Has a Horn

By Logan Kok, Josh Purdie and Addan Mahmood

Long, long ago before humans roamed the earth, only animals lived. One of those animals was Willy the wooly rhino. Willy lived in the Arctic tundra. The arctic tundra was a snowy white, luxurious, frosty home to hundreds and thousands of unique animal species. Willy wanted to stand out so he called a meeting with his friends to discuss how he could be unique.

Willy met with his friends Wolf, Eagle, Caribou and Bear at the big rock near the river. Willy asked them how he could become different. Caribou said, "You could have wings" Eagle replied, "I already have them."

"You could have antlers," said Wolf. Willy shook his head, "Caribou already has antlers." After an hour of brainstorming nobody could come up with any good ideas. They decided to meet at the rock at the same time tomorrow and then said their goodbyes.

Willy plodded home to his grove of evergreens. After a long deep sleep, he woke up in the morning feeling refreshed. He walked over to a tree and took a satisfying number two. When he finished, Willy skipped over to a patch of wildflowers and munched on them for a while. After that, he walked to the rock near the river feeling happy. When he got there, Wolf came running up to him short of breath and said "Help! Caribou is being attacked by the evil, savage Mammoth."

"Just follow Eagle, Bear is already on his way." Willy stampeded to help Caribou.

When Willy got there, he saw Caribou lying on the ground hurt and Bear being tossed around by the evil Mammoth. Willy charged in and smacked Mammoth in the side. Mammoth got knocked back but was still standing up. Willy followed up by head butting him in the back, but Mammoth was ready this time. He countered by swinging his tusk into Willy's nose. Mammoth pulled back to try to dislodge his tusk, but it was no use. Both of them tugged, and eventually, Mammoth's tusk came out of his face and got stuck in Willy's nose. He used the tusk to stab the mammoth and scare him away.   Willy's friends tried to pull it off, but it did not budge. The God Earth took pity on Willy and shaped the tusk into a horn. God Earth liked his new creation so much that he made all the rhinos in the world have these useful horns.   That is why all rhinos have horns.

Why the Lion Has a Big Mane

By Malik Eldebcan

In a land far away in Africa, there was a lion who had short hair. The lion was roaming and playing under a magic tree. This tree dripped black syrup into the lion's short hair. Suddenly, his hair began to grow while he played. He also played in the mud for fun, and the mixture of mud and leaves made his hair grow even longer and bushier. The lion loved his new look.

The lion lived alone, and nobody wanted to come near him because he looked scary with his big mane and cold stare. His hair kept growing and growing. His new mane made him look very powerful and strong. And this is why the lion has a beautiful mane.

في أرض بعيدة ان افريقيا يوجد اسد وشعره
قصير يلعب تحت   شجرة سرية وهذه الشجرة تنزل
عسل اسود على شعر الاسد وصباغة شعر الاسد ابتدا
ينمو و هو يلعب وكان يلعب في الطين للمتعة و مع
الخليط بين الطين والاوراق الشجر ابترا شعر الاسد ينمو
اطوال وتقيل وحب الاسد مظهره الجديد الاسد
كان يعيش لوحدة لا احد كاوز يقترب منه لا نه
شكله مخيف شعر الاسد ابتدا ينمو اطوال و اطوال
وهذا الشكل جعل الاسد قوي جدا وهذا السبب
جعل الاسد جميل وقوى

30

Why the Beaver Has a Dark Flat Tail

By Nini Li

Long ago before the sky had turned from dreamy green to hazy blue, a cheery beaver family lived by a large lake in Canada. There was a mommy beaver, a daddy beaver, and a little beaver named Rumania.

At that time, beavers didn't have flat, dark, coffee coloured tails; they had tails that were lengthy and incredibly shaggy. In fact, one of the beavers favourite past times was braiding the long hair on their tails.

Beavers all around had difficulties warning each other about danger because their shaggy tails were always really loose. They couldn't slap them hard, even if they braided them tightly. Their only other way to communicate and warn others was their shrieks, but the beaver's shrieks were never loud enough to alert other beaver in the area.

One day, Rumania was playing with her fish friends, Fishy, Flashy, Nissl, Lessee and her beaver friend, Rain. They were playing their beloved tag game. When Rain was it, Rumania jumped out of the water and ran on land. Rumania was darting across the edge of the lake with Rain racing right behind when she spotted a huge puddle of mud. She was too late to stop.

Rumania dropped into the huge puddle of muck and struggled to get back up. She went home immediately, and her mother took her to the family bathtub to soak her up. The mud on her tail was messed into her long hair, and it wouldn't dislodge at all. Mommy beaver got daddy beaver to help, but he couldn't make any progress either. Mommy and daddy beaver brought Rumania to the Great Tree of Sprits and Souls who knew almost everything. Perhaps he could help them.

The Great Tree told Rumania and her parents that there was only one way to get all of the icky muck off Rumania's tail, but her tail will probably never be able to have braids ever again. They tried to get it off anyways.

The wise tree picked up Rumania and swung her around while splashing her with water, but they quickly realized this mud wasn't regular mud. It didn't come off like the Great Tree said it would. Instead, it dried. Her tail was now dark, hard and round.

When Rumania grew up and had children, they had the same tail as Rumania. When Rumania's children grew up and had children, they also had hard, brown tails. This went on and on and on for generations. By the time the sky began to turn a beautiful hazy blue, all beavers had a hard, flat and dark brown tail.

Today beavers have a way to warn each other of danger. They slap their tails against the water to create a sound that can carry across the land. They live a much happier and safer life now thanks to Rumania's tail. And this is the story of why beavers have these beautiful dark flat tails.

Why the Spider is Feared

By Osher Stromberg, Tavin Lorenz and Caden Kutcher

Long ago in a faraway place called ancient Greece, there was a village in a mountain tree top forest. In this village, no one was frightened of any animal, and this was a problem. The people were out of control. Having some fear could be a good way to keep the people safe and out of trouble.

One day the Gods got mad because the people were not behaving. The Gods thought that perhaps their secret weapon, the spider, could scare the people enough to behave themselves. So the Gods gave the spider some extra legs, eight in total, to appear scarier and more powerful.

The Gods decide to put the eggs of the tiny orange spider in the people's water. The next day people started seeing the little orange house spider, but nobody was afraid of it. So the Gods started making venomous hairy eight legged spider beasts like the wolf spider, orb spider, and worst of all the tarantula. These scary spiders were seen over the next week. People got the spiders and threw them into the water but what the people didn't know was spiders could stay under water for many hours. The Gods had given these spiders magical powers to multiply when attacked in any way.

The next day the spiders were seen again, but this time there were more spiders and they were bigger. Every day the cycle repeated. The spiders were thrown in a bag and tossed in the river, but every day there were bigger and more spiders.

One day, a man named O'Brian wanted to destroy all the spiders. He was everyone's role model. When he went to kill all the spiders, as the villagers watched, the spiders surrounded O'Brian and bit him until he ran all the way back to the village. O'Brian admitted that he was terrified of the spiders and encourage the village people to follow the rules and behave. He felt this was a message from the Gods. The fear of another spider attack kept the village people well behaved and brought peace and harmony to the village.

And this is why the spider is still feared today.

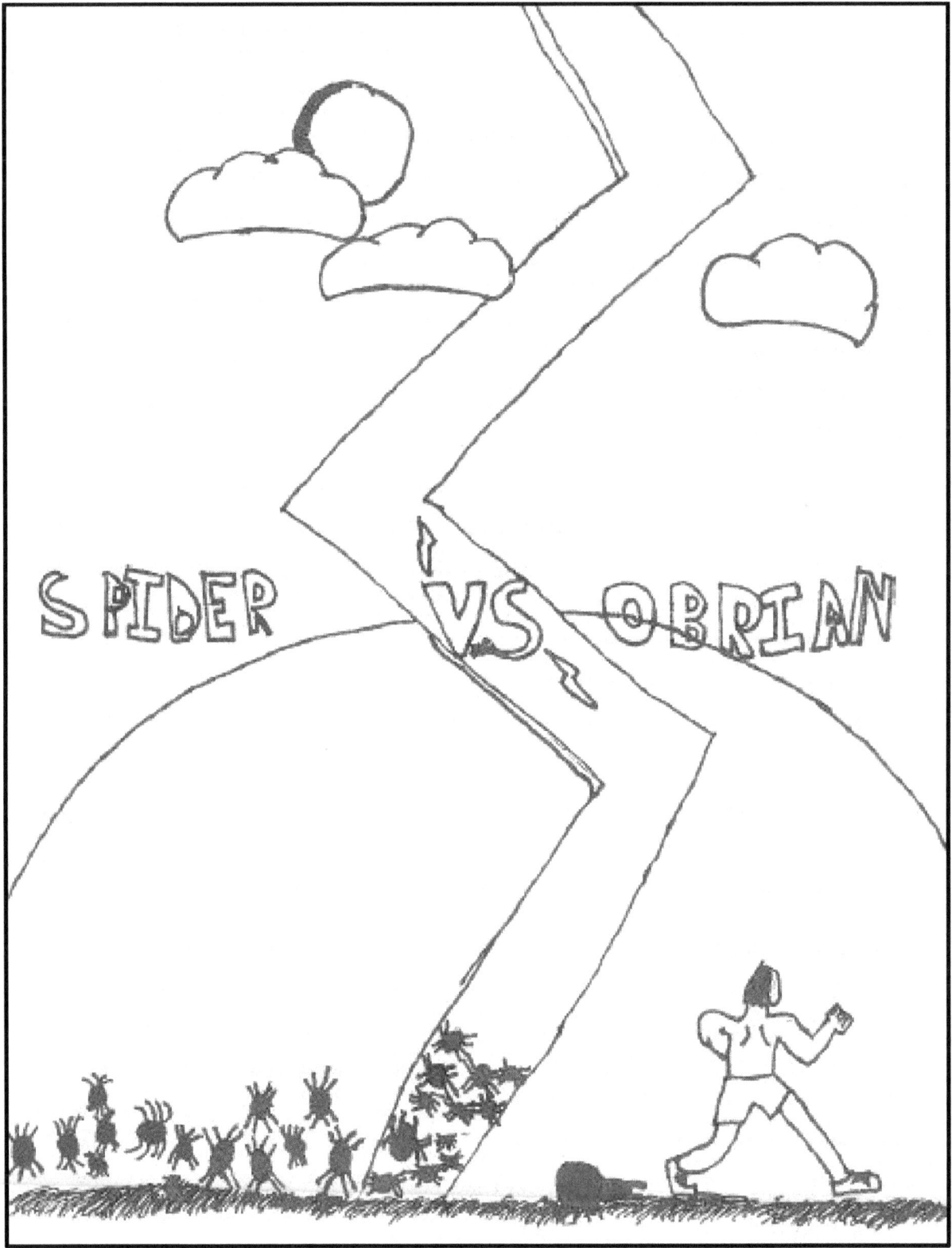

Why the Lion is King of the Jungle

By Usayd Ali

Long ago, there was a lion named Nike. He lived in a vast grassland where the sun was known to scorch the land. They called this land Africa.

The animals that lived there stayed in groups and looked out for one another. Every animal had a family or pair, except Nike. Nike would wander around the grassy, scorching land thinking about the things that bothered him. He felt that he was weak and he wanted to feel more courageous. Nike often starved because he was too scared to try and get his prey. He thought they would attack him back and hurt him very badly. He was afraid to be fierce.

One day Nike was walking around a tree when he heard growling and other sounds. He looked behind the tree and saw two tigers and three snakes staring at him in hunger. As they approached, Nike started trembling in fear. He thought about running, but he was so frightened he couldn't even move a muscle. However, doing nothing was even scarier, so he just let go of his fear and started running for his life. He couldn't believe it, but he actually outran the animals who chased him.

The next day Nike was walking through the jungle again. Suddenly he noticed several tigers and snakes surrounding him. Again, Nike wanted to run or do something, but he was too afraid. He wanted to tell them to leave him alone, but he couldn't even raise his voice.

Inside his head, he heard voices reminding him that the tigers and other animals had taken his parents away from him. Nike was getting worked up and furious. He started growling and let all his anger and fear out at once!

ROOAARR!!!!!

The tigers and other animals backed up and started running away. From this day forward, when Nike passes other animals they always back up in fear of him. And this is why the lion in now considered King of the Jungle.